Barry Hines & Allan Stronach

THE PLAY OF
<u>KES</u>

**Introduction and activities by
Anne Fenton**

Heinemann is an imprint of Pearson Education Limited,
a company incorporated in England and Wales, having
its registered office at Edinburgh Gate, Harlow, Essex, CM20 2JE.
Registered company number: 872828

Heinemann is a registered trademark of Pearson Education Limited

Series Editor: Lawrence Till

First published in the *Heinemann Plays* series by
Heinemann Educational Ltd in 1993

A catalogue record for this book is available from the British
Library on request.

ISBN: 978 0 435232 88 7

22

13

Cover design by Keith Pointing

Designed by Jeffrey White Creative Associates

Typeset by Taurus Graphics, Kidlington, Oxon

Printed in China (CTPS / 22)

CONTENTS

INTRODUCTION

Written by one of Yorkshire's most celebrated writers, *Kes* is the story of 15-year-old Billy Casper, the boy with nowhere to go and nothing to say, with problems with family and school. When neither school nor family have offered him anything, the kestrel hawk is his only companion, and the focus of the loving relationship he has always been denied. Billy showers his affection and skill on the bird which, like himself, is trained but not tamed, and will either destroy or be destroyed.

Barry Hines was born in the mining village of Hoyland Common, near Barnsley in 1939. He was educated at Ecclesfield Grammar School, where his main achievement was to be selected for the England Grammar Schools' football team. On leaving school, he worked as an Apprentice Mining Surveyor and played football for Barnsley, before entering Loughborough Training College to study Physical Education. He taught for several years in London and South Yorkshire before becoming a full-time novelist and playwright.

Barry Hines' novels include: *The Blinder, A Kestrel for a Knave, First Signs, The Gamekeeper, The Price of Coal, Looks and Smiles* and *Unfinished Business. A Kestrel for a Knave* (written in 1968 and on which *Kes* is based) is concerned with Hines' own experiences while growing up and as a teacher. He and his brother kept various wild animals as Billy did, including a kestrel chick which they took from a nest high up in a ruined hall and trained. Barry Hines says of his work:

'My novels are mostly about working-class life. They are about people who live on council estates or in small terraced houses. The men work in mines and steelworks, the women in underpaid menial jobs – or, increasingly, are on the dole. I feel a strong sense of social injustice on behalf of these people which stems from my own mining background. The hardness and danger of that life (my grandfather was killed down the pit, my father was injured several times) formed my attitudes and made me a socialist.

My political viewpoint is the mainspring of my work. It fuels my energy, which is fine, as long as the characters remain believable and do not degenerate into dummies merely mouthing my own beliefs. However, I would rather risk being didactic than lapsing into blandness – or end up writing novels about writers writing novels. If that happens it will be time to hang up the biro.'

Barry's cinema, radio and television credits include *Kes*, *Looks and Smiles* (Prix du Cinema Contemporaine, Cannes 1981), *Billy's Last Stand, Speech Day, Two Men from Derby, The Price of Coal, The Gamekeeper, A Question of Leadership, Threads, Shooting Stars* and *Born Kicking.*

In 1969 *A Kestrel for a Knave* was turned into a highly successful film (now available on video), directed by Ken Loach with a cast of local actors and starring the 15-year-old David Bradley as Billy Casper.

Barry Hines worked on the screenplay with the director and the producer Tony Garnett. It had a tight eight-week shooting schedule and was filmed entirely in Barnsley. The showing in the North broke box office records and it was then shown at the Academy Cinema in London and in Cannes.

The play

Kes, the play, grew from the need of a group of school students to find a contemporary play they could not only perform but also associate with. Having read the novel they were already able to sympathise with many of the situations and characters in the story of *Kes*.

The resulting play is intentionally episodic presenting in 23 scenes aspects of the life of Billy Casper during his final months at school. Initially it is the story of a boy obtaining and training a kestrel hawk but it is about much more as well. It is not the training of the hawk that is the important thing in the relationship between boy and bird but rather the attitude that Billy has towards Kes that makes him able to train it. More than anything it is an attitude of respect, admiration and affection.

Attitude is also the theme with which other aspects of the play are concerned. As well as his attitude to Kes it is also about Billy Casper's attitudes towards the people he knows and meets and about their attitudes towards him.

We see the Casper household and attitudes between Billy, Mrs Casper and step-brother Jud on four occasions. Billy's only real attempt at conversation with his family, when he begins to tell his mother of his plan to get a kestrel and build a hut for it, is quickly dismissed when she realises she is late for her evening out.

During the scenes when Billy is at school we are able to see the attitudes of both his superiors and his peers. Only on three short occasions is he given any real consideration by anyone who represents the school system. Mr Farthing, the English teacher, twice attempts a conversation with Billy personally and is partially successful each time. The third, and most successful occasion that the school has anything to offer is when – once again encouraged by Farthing – Billy is able to hold the full attention of the class as he relates, through his experiences, how he first 'obtained' and then trained Kes.

Apart from these three occasions the school not only has nothing to offer Billy but through its refusal to admit as much repeatedly rebukes him from all sides. His classmates spend much time poking fun at him because he has strayed from the norm and prefers the company of Kes to that of his peer group.

The Headmaster, even with a full 30 years' teaching experience behind him, administers the cane rather than attempt to discover the reason why Billy fell asleep during morning assembly. Sugden, the P.E. teacher, using the double weapon of sarcasm and authority, gives Billy a miserable time during the games lesson. Even the Youth Employment Officer becomes easily exasperated with the realisation that not only has the school been unable to offer Billy anything but neither can he.

Billy Casper stands, of course, as a representative of a significant proportion of our school populace today. He is even more representative because at the end of it all he merely resigns himself to the facts. Billy Casper, however, has the advantage over the majority in that he has been able to experience something that neither home nor school could offer him. In having known and trained Kes he has had something to both admire and respect.

Barry Hines writes about the play:

'I once went to give a reading in a school in Lincolnshire. As I was sitting in the staffroom waiting to go and meet a group of students, a teacher said to me, "You know that book you wrote, *Kes*?" I said, "Yes". He said "Did you write it by accident? Or did you write it on purpose?" I didn't know what to say and still don't. How you write a novel, or a play, or anything come to that, by accident is beyond me. Anyway, whatever he meant, *Kes* was certainly no accident. In fact, it's probably the least accidental thing I've written. I'd been building up to it for a long time.

Kes is about education, not falconry. It's a story about a boy not a bird. I think that's why the novel translates so effectively to the stage. You don't have to see the kestrel to appreciate Billy Casper's troubles. His problems are concerned with family and school. The kestrel is a symbol of Billy's potential. Through the hawk, we seek what he is capable of, and this element of the play works just as strongly in the imagination as if seen.'

The first production

The original production of *Kes* was staged at Colley School, Sheffield with a cast of 30 males and 17 females.

The play is made up of a large number of short separate scenes. Little or no scenery as such is required as each scene can be adequately represented by the use of a few basic and obvious props. In the original production three main acting areas were used. The open area of the traditional stage was used for most of the scenes but two recurring scenes were staged in front of the proscenium, the part of the stage between the curtain and the orchestra. To stage right an acting area was built representing the Casper household while to stage left one was constructed to represent the backyard of the Casper house including the hut for Kes.

With 23 scenes, continuity is an important aspect of any production. The triple staging was the major factor in ensuring this as Billy Casper, seen in every scene, moved from one acting area to another. Also contributing to the continuity in the original production, however, was a series of specially produced slides projected on to a screen to one side of the stage. Used between most of the scenes these were more than just a theatrical device to fill a series of small gaps. Besides this they were able to complement the action by echoing the events or setting of the previous scene or beginning to establish some kind of mood for what was to follow.

They showed such things as the street where Billy lived, the outside of the library that he visited, the newsagent's shop, a close-up of Billy's books and various pictures of the inside of the school.

The role of the kestrel, being central to much of the action in the story, is as important as ever. However, to present Billy Casper's kestrel either as a real bird or depicted on film or slides – all within the realms of possibility – is going to add little to a production. The strength of the kestrel lies in its influence on Billy Casper and the attitude of the boy to the bird. Consequently, rather than the process of capture and training, it is Billy Casper's attitude and respect towards the bird that a production should concentrate on establishing. It is perhaps significant that one of the most influential characters in twentieth-century drama in Samuel Beckett's *Waiting for Godot* makes no appearance at all.

The contemporary nature of the subject matter of *Kes* means that the play lends itself a great deal to improvisation either as preparation for a production or as a group activity with no end except participation. There are many characters in the play whose attitudes are worth considering. Improvisation can often lead not only to the recognition of a particular attitude but also to discovery and discussion concerning how that particular attitude may have arisen in the first place.

In preparation for the original production greater understanding of the various attitudes was gained by occasionally exchanging characters. Much time was spent on allowing the characters to tell Billy Casper what they thought of him and why, and vice versa. More importantly, perhaps, was that on some occasions Billy Casper exchanged roles with Sugden, or Gryce or even Jud. Interaction of characters in this way led not only to a more worthwhile understanding of the story but, far more importantly as far as *Kes* is concerned, to a deeper understanding of the characters involved and the attitudes that they hold.

Questions and Explorations

At the end of the play text, you will find ideas for follow up work. The first section, 'Keeping Track', can be followed scene-by-scene as you read the play and contains questions to help you think clearly about the action in each scene. The second section, 'Explorations', has extended activities to help you think more broadly about the characters, themes and issues in the play as a whole. There are also some activities which will help you prepare for putting on a performance of the play.

Cast of First Production

The original production of *Kes* was presented at Colley School, Sheffield in April 1974 with the following cast:

Bill Colton
Paul Allender
Kim Beatson
Steven Hawley
Michael Tyson
Ian Aldridge
Albert Nelson
Rosemary Barr
Diane Stephenson
Stephanie Wilson
Frank Brightmore
David Burns
Steven Cartledge
Michael Holmes
Shaun Allen
Alex Morton
Paul Timmins
Steven Martin
Andrew Camm
Terry Connolly
Kevin Fox
Adrian Onerearnshaw
John Delamore
Glyn Gibbs

Philip Rogers
Gary Palmer
Karen Bream
Alan Jackson
Philip Baker
Jayne Salisbury
John Bellamy
Nigel Holmes
Douglas Gilberthorpe
Alison Manning
Linda Goodwin
Jasmine Peacock
Vicki Mackley
Maureen Brown
Fiona Worthington
David Spillings
Trevor Bradshaw
Darrell Hepworth
Tina Hattersley
Sylvia Spillings
Christine Thompson
Jayne Saxton
Cheryl Woodruff

List of Characters

Billy Casper

Jud

Mr Porter

Man in shop

Milkman

Mrs Casper

Mrs MacDowall

Farmer

Librarian

Mr Gryce

MacDowall

Mr Crossley

1st smoker

2nd smoker

Messenger

Mr Farthing

Anderson

Tibbut

Holmes

Cartledge

Baker

Barr

Martin

Allen

Mr Sugden

Palmer

Mrs Rose

Man at bookmakers

Mr Beal

Gibbs

Delamore

Rogers

Mrs Allender

Allender

Youth Employment Officer

ACT ONE

Scene 1

Billy and Jud's bedroom and kitchen.

Billy and Jud are asleep in the same bed. Quiet. The alarm clock rings. Billy fumbles for it, eventually finds it and switches it off.

Billy   Bloody thing.

(*Pause*)

Jud!

(*Pause*)

Jud   What?

Billy   You'd better get up.

(*Pause*)

Alarm's gone off you know.

Jud   Think I don't know?

(*Pause*)

Billy   Jud.

Jud   What?

Billy   You'll be late.

Jud   Oh, shut it.

Billy   Clock's gone off you know.

Jud   I said 'shut it!'

(*He thumps Billy.*)

Billy   Gi'oer, that hurts.

Jud   Well shut it then.

Billy   I'll tell mi' mam about you.

Jud slowly gets out of bed. He finally finds his trousers and puts them on.

Billy   Set alarm for me Jud. For seven.

1

Jud	It's nearly that now.
Billy	It's not.
Jud	It's late. Clock's wrong.
	He pulls the bedclothes off Billy.
Billy	You rotten sod.
Jud	Get up then.
	Jud goes into the kitchen for breakfast. He finds himself some bread and jam on the table. Billy slowly gets dressed and joins him. He looks at the clock in the kitchen.
Billy	Have you seen the time?
Jud	7 o'clock gone.
Billy	You're late.
Jud	Hour and half.
	Jud pours himself a cup of tea. He drains the pot which means there is none for Billy.
Billy	Smashing morning again.
Jud	You wouldn't be saying that if you were going where I'm going.
Billy	Just think, when I'm doing 'papers you'll be going down in the cage.
Jud	Yeah. And just think, in a few weeks you'll be coming down wi' me.
Billy	I'll not.
Jud	Won't you?
Billy	No, because I'm not going to work down the pit.
Jud	Where you going to work then?
	Billy has a drink of milk from the bottle.
Billy	I don't know, but I'm not going to work down the pit.
Jud	No, and shall I tell you why?
	(He puts his jacket on.)
	For one thing, you've to be able to read and write

before they'll let you down the pit. And for another, they wouldn't have a weedy little bugger like you.

Jud goes out. He has left his 'snap' on the table. Billy eventually sees it, opens it and begins to eat one of the sandwiches. He is half-way through it when Jud returns.

Jud I've forgot my snap.

(*Billy finishes off the sandwich, gets up and hurries off to his paper round.*)

I'll murder you when I get home. And don't bother with your bike – I've already got it.

Scene 2

Mr Porter's newsagent shop.

Mr Porter is carefully arranging newspapers on the counter when Billy enters.

Mr Porter I thought you weren't coming.

Billy Why, I'm not late am I?

(*Porter looks at his pocket watch.*)

I nearly was though.

Mr Porter What do you mean?

Billy Late. Our Jud went to the pit on my bike.

Mr Porter What you going to do then?

Billy Walk it.

Mr Porter And how long do you think that's going to take you?

Billy Not long.

Mr Porter Some folks like to read their papers the day they come out, you know.

Billy It'll not take me that much longer. I've done it before.

Mr Porter 'Cos there's a waiting list a mile long, you know, for your job. Grand lads as well some of them, from up Firs Hill and round there.

Billy	What's up. I haven't let you down have I?

A man on his way to work enters the shop. Mr Porter's attitude changes immediately.

Mr Porter	Morning Sir. Nice again.
Man	Twenty Players please.
Mr Porter	Certainly Sir. Thank you.

The man pays and goes out.

Mr Porter	You know what they said when I took you on don't you? They said – 'you'll have to keep your eyes open now, you know, 'cos they're all alike off that estate. They'll take your breath if you're not careful.'
Billy	I've never taken anything of yours, have I?
Mr Porter	Never had chance, that's why.
Billy	I've stopped getting into trouble now.
Mr Porter	Come on then, you'll be wanting me to take them round for you next.

(He climbs a ladder to begin stacking things on the shelves.)

Billy	What time is it?
Mr Porter	A quarter to eight.
Billy	Already?

(He squeezes past the ladder to get his pile of newspapers from behind the counter.)

Mr Porter	You'll be late for school. Mind you, I wouldn't like to think it was my job trying to learn you 'owt.

Billy squeezes past the ladder again and shakes it on purpose.

Billy	Look out, Mr Porter. You're all right, I've got you.
Mr Porter	You clumsy young bugger. What you trying to do? Kill me?
Billy	I lost my balance.
Mr Porter	I wouldn't put it past you either.

(Descends ladder and feels his heart.)

I fair felt my heart go then.

Billy	Are you all right now, Mr Porter?
Mr Porter	All right? Aye, bloody champion.
Billy	I'll be off then.
Mr Porter	And don't be late for tonight's.

Scene 3

Billy meets the milkman.

The milkman is about to deliver two pints of milk to a house.

Milkman	How's it going then, young 'un?

Billy stops and leans.

Billy	Oh, not so bad.
Milkman	You could do wi' some transport. That milk float's better than walking you know.
Billy	Ay, only just, though. They only go five miles an hour them things.
Milkman	Still better than walking though.
Billy	I could go faster on a kid's scooter.
Milkman	You know what I always say?
Billy	What?
Milkman	Third class riding's better than first class walking any day.
Billy	I'm not so sure with one of them things.
Milkman	Please yourself. See yer.
Billy	See yer.

Scene 4

Billy's house.

Billy enters the house and puts his paper-round bag away.

Mrs Casper	Oh, it's you Billy. Haven't you gone to school yet?
Billy	Brought my bag back.
	Mrs Casper picks up an empty cigarette packet.
Mrs Casper	You've not got a fag on you have you?
	(*He doesn't reply.*)
	There's tea mashed if you want a cup. I don't know if there's any milk left.
	Billy goes to pour himself a cup of tea, but there is none left.
Mrs Casper	Do me a favour love, and run to the shop for some cigarettes.
Billy	They'll not be open yet.
Mrs Casper	You can go to the back door. Mr Hardy'll not mind.
Billy	I can't. I'll be late.
Mrs Casper	Go on love, bring a few things back with you.
Billy	Go yourself.
Mrs Casper	I've no time. Just tell him to put it in the book and I'll pay him at the weekend.
Billy	He says you can't have anything until you've paid up.
Mrs Casper	He always says that. I'll give you 5p when you come back.
Billy	Don't want 5p. I'm off.
Mrs Casper	Come here, will you?
Billy	I'm not Mam, I'll be late for school.
Mrs Casper	Just you wait till tonight. An' there's a bet of our Jud's to take an' all. Don't forget that.
Billy	I'm not taking it.
Mrs Casper	You'd better lad.
Billy	I'm fed up taking 'em. He can take it himself.
Mrs Casper	How can he when he's not back home in time?
Billy	I don't care, I'm not taking it. I'm off.
Mrs Casper	You just wait. You'll see.

Scene 5

Mac's house.

Billy throws pebbles up to the window of MacDowall's house.

Billy   Mac. Mac.

Mrs MacDowall comes to the window and leans out.

She pulls her dressing-gown tight as it is cold.

Billy   Is he up?

Mrs MacDowall   What do you want at this time?

Billy   Is your Mac up?

Mrs MacDowall   Course he's not up, this time on a Saturday.

Billy   Isn't he getting up?

Mrs MacDowall   Not that I know of. He's fast asleep.

Billy   He's a right 'un. We're going bird nesting. It was his idea.

Mrs MacDowall   Stop shouting will you?

Billy   He's not coming then?

Mrs MacDowall   No, he's not. You'd better come back after dinner if you want to see him.

(She closes the window. Billy throws a handful of dirt at it and Mrs MacDowall reappears.)

Bugger off you little sod.

Billy goes bird nesting by himself.

Scene 6

Watching a kestrel.

Billy is sitting watching a kestrel that has been collecting food for its young, which are nesting in an old monastery wall. The farmer, who the field belongs to, appears.

Farmer	Hey. What are you doing?
Billy	Nothing.
Farmer	Go on then. Don't you know this is private property?
Billy	No! Can I get up to that kestrel's nest?
Farmer	What kestrel's nest?
Billy	Up that wall.
Farmer	There's no nest up there, son.
Billy	There is. I've just been watching it fly in.
	(*Pause*)
Farmer	And what you going to do when you get up to it? Take all the eggs?
Billy	There's no eggs in, they're young 'uns.
Farmer	Then there's nothing to get up for then is there?
Billy	I just wanted to look, that's all.
Farmer	And you'd be looking from six feet under if you tried to climb up there.
Billy	Can I just have a look from the bottom then? I've never found a hawk's nest before. That's where it is, look, in that hole in the side of that window.
Farmer	I know it is, it's nested here donkey's years now.
Billy	Just think, and I never knew.
Farmer	There's not many that does.
Billy	I've been watching them from across in the wood. You ought to have seen them. One of them was sat on that telegraph pole for ages. I was right underneath it, then I saw its mate. It came from miles away and started to hover just over there. Then it dived down behind that wall and came up with something in its claws. You ought to have seen it mister.
Farmer	I see it every day. It always sits on that pole.
Billy	I wish I could see it every day. Has anybody ever been up that wall to look?
Farmer	Not that I know of. It's dangerous. They've been

	going to pull it down for ages.
Billy	I bet I could get up.
Farmer	You're not going to have the chance though.
Billy	If I lived here I'd get a young 'un and train it.
Farmer	Would you?
	(*Pause*)
Billy	You can train them.
Farmer	And how would you go about it?
	(*Pause*)
Billy	Do you know?
Farmer	No, and there's not many that does. That's why I won't let anyone near, because if they can't be kept properly it's criminal.
Billy	Do you know anyone who's kept one?
Farmer	One or two. Not many.
Billy	Where could you find out about them?
Farmer	Books I suppose. I should think there are books on falconry.
Billy	Think there'll be any in the library?
Farmer	Could be in the City library. They've books on everything there.
Billy	I'm off now then. So long mister.
	(*Billy runs off.*)
Farmer	Hey!
Billy	What?
Farmer	Go through that gate. Not over the wall.

Scene 7

The public library.
The librarian is sitting at her desk. Others are looking at the bookshelves. Billy enters.

Billy	Got any books on hawks missis?
Librarian	Hawks?
Billy	I want a book on falconry.
Librarian	I'm not sure. You'd better try under ornithology.
Billy	What's that?
Librarian	Under zoology.
	Billy goes to look for the shelf.
Librarian	Hey!
Billy	What?
Librarian	Are you a member?
Billy	What do you mean, a member?
Librarian	A member of the library.
Billy	I don't know owt about that. I just want a book on falconry. That's all.
Librarian	You can't borrow books unless you're a member.
Billy	I only want one.
Librarian	Have you filled one of these forms in?
	(Billy shakes head.)
	Well, you're not a member then. Do you live in the Borough?
Billy	What do you mean?
Librarian	The Borough, the City!
Billy	No, I live on the Valley estate.
Librarian	Well that's in the Borough isn't it?
	A customer has a book stamped out. Billy just stands looking round in the library.
Billy	Can I get a book now then?
Librarian	You'll have to take one of these forms home first for your father to sign.
Billy	My dad's away.
Librarian	You'll have to wait till he comes home then.
Billy	I don't mean away like that. I mean he's left home.

Librarian	Oh, I see . . . well in that case your mother'll have to sign it.
Billy	She's at work.
Librarian	She can sign it when she comes home, can't she?
Billy	She'll not be home till tea time and it's Sunday tomorrow. I want a book today.
Librarian	Then you'll just have to wait, won't you?
Billy	Just let me go an' see'f you've got one, an' if you have I'll sit down at one o' them tables and read it.
Librarian	You can't. You're not a member.
Billy	Nobody'll know.
Librarian	It's against the rules.
Billy	Go on. I'll bring you this paper back on Monday then.

Another customer hands a book to the librarian to be stamped out. They chat pleasantly about the weather. Billy sees the zoology shelf and goes to it. He quickly finds a book about hawks, puts it under his jacket and quickly goes out of the library, past the two still talking at the desk.

Billy	Ta-ra.

Scene 8

Billy's house.

Billy is quietly reading the book from the library when Jud enters.

He is getting ready to go out for the night.

Jud	What do you want that for, when you can't read? *(Snatches the book from him.)*
Billy	Give it me back. Come here.
Jud	Falconry? What do you know about falconry?
Billy	Give it me back.

Jud	'A Falconer's Handbook'. Where have you got this from?
Billy	I've lent it.
Jud	Nicked it more like. Where have you got it from?
Billy	The library in town.
Jud	You must be cracked.
Billy	How do you mean?
Jud	Nicking books. I could understand it if it was money but chuff me, not a book.
Billy	I've been reading it all afternoon. I'm nearly half-way through.
Jud	And what better off will you be when you've read it?
Billy	A lot because I'm going to get a young kestrel and train it.
Jud	You couldn't train a flea. Anyroad, where you goin' to get a kestrel from?
Billy	I know a nest.
Jud	You don't.
Billy	All right then I don't.
Jud	Where is it?
Billy	I'm not telling.
Jud	I said where?
	(*Pushes Billy's face into cushion and puts his arm up his back.*)
	Where?
Billy	Give over Jud, you're breaking my arm.
Jud	Where, then?
Billy	Monastery farm.
	(*Jud lets go.*)
Jud	I'll have to see about going round there with my gun.
Billy	I'll tell the farmer if you do, he protects them.
Jud	Protects them. Don't talk wet. Hawks are a menace to farmers, they eat all their poultry and everything.

Billy	I know, they dive down on their cows and carry them away an' all.
Jud	Funny bugger.
Billy	Well, you talk daft. How big do you think they are? Kestrels only eat insects and mice and little birds sometimes.
Jud	You think you know something about them don't you?
Billy	I know more about them than you anyroad.
Jud	You ought to an' all. You nearly live round in them woods. It's a wonder you don't turn into a wild man.

(*Jud scratches his armpits and runs round the room imitating a wildman.*)

Billy Casper, wild man of the woods. I ought to have you in a cage, I'd make a bloody fortune.

Billy	I was laid watching them for hours this afternoon.
Jud	I'm hoping I'll be laid watching a bird tonight, but she won't have feathers on.
Billy	You ought to have seen them though Jud.

(*Jud is tying his tie.*)

Jud	A few pints first.
Billy	You ought to have seen them dive down.
Jud	Then straight across to the club.

Mrs Casper enters.

Mrs Casper	You're a couple of noisy buggers. What you tormenting him for Jud?
Jud	I never touched him.
Billy	Not much. He nearly broke my arm, that's all.
Jud	I'll break your neck next time.
Mrs Casper	Oh shut it both of you.
Jud	Well he's nothing but a big baby.
Billy	And you're nothing but a big bully.
Mrs Casper	I said shut it.

(Pause)

Where you going tonight then?

Jud Usual I suppose.

Mrs Casper And don't be coming home drunk again. Seen my shoes Billy love?

(Jud is looking into the mirror.)

Jud Some bird's going to be lucky tonight.

(He goes out.)

(Mrs Casper is picking her shoes up.)

Mrs Casper They could have done with a polish. Still, never mind, it'll soon be dark. There's no ladders in these stockings is there Billy?

(Billy speaks without looking.)

Billy Can't see any.

Mrs Casper What you going to do with yourself tonight love?

Billy Read my book.

Mrs Casper That's nice. What's it about?

Billy Falconry. I'm going to get a young kestrel and train it.

Mrs Casper That's nice. I say, what time is it?

Billy I've cleaned the bottom shed out ready, an' I've built a little nesting box out of an orange box, 'til . . .

Mrs Casper Ten to eight. I'm going to be late as usual. Here, there's 10p for you. Go and buy yourself some pop and crisps or something. Ta-ra.

Billy reads aloud but hesitantly. It is important to hear him struggling with the language.

Billy The kestrel is about 12–14 inches long. The male is slightly smaller than the female and both sexes have reddish-chestnut plumage with black spots on their upper parts and buff plumage with brownish streaks below. In level flight the kestrel has a silhouette typical of the falcons: a large head, broad shoulders, long pointed wings and quite a long tail. It can hover in the air for minutes on end when hunting. When it is doing so its tail is fanned and its head is inclined downwards. It lives in many different types of places: mountains and hills, open moors, farmland, suburbs and even city centres on occasions.

Lights fade.

Scene 9

Jud returns home.

Billy is now in bed reading the book to himself when he hears Jud come into the house. He switches off the bedside lamp and pretends to be asleep. Jud enters. He is drunk.

Jud Billy. Billy.

(*He is swaying gently.*)

Are you ashleep Billy?

(*He begins to get undressed, humming a pop tune he has been hearing all night while still gently swaying. He tries to take off his trousers but begins to lose balance.*)

Whoa you bugger, whoa. Billy wake up. Billy.

(*Pulls at bedclothes.*)

Wake up Billy I said.

Billy Give over Jud, I'm asleep.

Jud Help me get undressh Billy. I'm drunk. I'm too drunk to get undreshed.

(*He drops on to the bed giggling.*)

Help me Billy.

Billy gets out of bed and takes Jud's trousers off for him.

Billy I'm fed up of this game. It's every Saturday night alike.

(*Jud snores loudly.*)

Just like a pig snoring – a drunken pig – Jud the drunken pig. He stinks. You stink. Jud the stinking, drunken pig.

(*He shuts Jud's mouth.*)

Jud What's a matter? What's a matter?

Billy Go back to sleep you pig—hog—sow—drunken bastard.

(*He starts tapping Jud.*)

Pig—hog—sow—drunk—ken—bas—tard.

(*He repeats this and as the chant gets louder, so the slaps get harder.*)

Billy Pig—hog—sow—drunk—ken—bas—tard.
Pig—hog—sow—drunk—ken—bas—tard.

He eventually thumps Jud who makes a loud noise and tries to sit up. Billy grabs his own trousers and runs out of the bedroom.

Scene 10

Morning assembly.

The classes come into the School Hall noisily, accompanied by various members of staff. When Mr Gryce comes on to the platform they immediately go quiet.

Gryce Hymn No. 175 – 'New Every Morning is the Love'.

(*They begin turning pages, coughing, making a fuss, etc.*)

Stop that infernal coughing! It's every morning alike. As soon as the hymn is announced you're off.

(*Pause. Then a lone voice coughs.*)

Who did that? I said who did that.

(*No one owns up.*)

Mr Crossley. Somewhere near you. Didn't you see the boy?

              (*Crossley pushes his way into the lines.*)
              There Crossley! That's where it came from! Around there!
              (*Crossley grabs hold of MacDowall.*)

MacDowall   It wasn't me sir.

Crossley   Of course it was you.

MacDowall   It wasn't sir, honest.

Crossley   Don't argue lad, I saw you.

Gryce   MacDowall. I might have known it was you. Get to my room lad.

              (*MacDowall leaves the hall.*)
              Right. We'll try again. Hymn 175.

              (*They sing the first verse very poorly.*)

Gryce   Stop! And what is that noise supposed to represent? I've heard sweeter sounds in a slaughter house! This is supposed to be a hymn of joy – not a dirge. If that's the best you can do, we won't bother. The whole school will therefore return to this hall after school is over. Then you'll sing. Or I'll MAKE you sing like you've never sung before. We'll now say the Lord's Prayer. Heads Bowed. Our Father . . .

              (*The school join in the Lord's Prayer. After it is finished Gryce tells them to sit down. Billy who is day-dreaming about being with Kes does not hear him and so remains standing.*)

Gryce   Casper. Casper.

              (*Billy opens his eyes and sits down.*)
              Up Casper. Up on your feet lad. Silence!
              (*Pause*)
              You were asleep, weren't you?

Billy   I don't know sir.

Gryce   Well I know. You were fast asleep weren't you? Fast asleep during the Lord's Prayer. Were you tired lad?

Billy   I don't know sir.

Gryce   Don't know? You wouldn't be tired if you got to bed at night instead of sitting up till dawn watching some tripe on television. Report to my room now. You will be tired when I've finished with you.

(Billy goes.)

Gryce   There will be a meeting of the intermediate football team in the gym at break this morning. A reminder that the Youth Employment Officer will be in this afternoon to see the Easter leavers. You all know the time of your appointments. Be there. Finally I would like to see the three members of the smokers' union whom I didn't have time to deal with yesterday. They can pay their dues at my room after assembly. Right, dismiss.

Scene 11

Headmaster's study.

The three smokers, Billy and MacDowall are waiting for the headmaster to return.

MacDowall   It wasn't me that coughed you know. I'm going to tell Gryce that an' all.

1st smoker   It makes no difference whether you tell him or not, he doesn't listen.

MacDowall   I'll bring my father up if he gives me the stick anyway.

Billy   What you always bringing your father up for? He never does anything when he comes. They say last time he came up, Gryce gave him stick as well.

MacDowall   At least I've got a proper father to bring up, that's more than you can say Casper.

Billy   Shut your gob, MacDowall.

MacDowall   Why, what you going to do about it?

Billy   You'd be surprised.

MacDowall   Right then, I'll see you at break.

Billy	Anytime you want.
MacDowall	Right then.
Billy	Right.

Pause. A small boy enters with a message for Gryce.

1st smoker	If you've come for the stick you'd better get to the back of the queue.
Messenger	I've not come for the stick; Crossley's sent me with a message.

Pause.

MacDowall	It's his favourite trick this. He likes to keep you waiting. He thinks it makes it worse.

(2nd smoker takes cigarettes, etc. out of his pocket and goes to the boy.)

2nd smoker	Here, you'd better save us these until after. If he searches us he'll only take them off us and give us another two strokes.
Messenger	I don't want them, you're not getting me into trouble as well.
2nd smoker	Who's getting you into trouble? You can give them back after.

(Messenger shakes head.)

Messenger	Don't want them.
2nd smoker	Do you want some fist instead?

The three smokers surround him and fill his pockets with cigarettes, lighters, etc.

Billy	Hey! He's here. Gryce Pudding.

Gryce enters. Boys stand in a line.

Gryce	Right you reprobates.

(They go in.)

The same old faces. Why is it always the same old faces?

Messenger	Please sir.
Gryce	Don't interrupt boy, when I'm speaking.

(He walks down the line.)

I'm sick of you boys, you'll be the death of me. Not a day goes by without me having to see a line of boys. I can't remember a day – not one day – in all the years that I've been in this school, and how long's that? . . . ten years, and the school is no better now than it was on the day it opened. I can't understand it, I really can't.

(He goes to the window and admires the neatly cut lawns outside. He remains there as he continues talking.)

I thought I understood young people. I should be able to with all my experience – I've taught in this city thirty-five years now – but there's something happening today that's frightening. It makes me feel that it's all been a waste of time.

(The boys look at each other, bored.)

Like it's a waste of time talking to you boys now, because you're not taking a blind bit of notice of what I'm saying. I know what you're thinking now, you're thinking why doesn't he shut up and get on with it. That's what you're thinking isn't it? Isn't it MacDowall?

MacDowall   No sir.

Gryce   Of course it is. I can see it in your eyes lad, they're glazed over.

Messenger   Please sir.

Gryce   Shut up lad. As far as I can see there's been no advance at all in discipline, decency, manners or morals. And do you know how I know this? Because I still have to use this every day.

(He takes the cane from the top of his desk.)

I can understand why we had to use it back in the 'twenties and 'thirties. Those were hard times, they bred hard people and it needed hard measures to deal with them. We knew where we stood in those days; they bred people with respect for a start. Even today a man will stop me in the street and say – 'Hello Mr Gryce, remember me?' And we'll pass away the time of day and he'll laugh about the thrashings I used to give him.

(*The boys have stopped listening altogether by now.*)

They took it then, but not now. Not in this day of the common man, when every boy quotes his rights and shoots off home for his father as soon as I look at him . . . No guts . . . no backbone . . . you've nothing to commend you whatsoever.

(*He swishes the stick in front of him.*)

So for want of a better solution I continue using the cane, knowing full well that you'll be back time and time again for some more. You smokers will carry on smoking just the same.

(*One of the smokers is smirking at the other boys.*)

Yes you can smirk lad. I bet your pockets are ladened up in readiness for break this very moment, aren't they? Aren't they? Well just empty them, come on, get your pockets emptied.

The three smokers, Billy and MacDowall begin to empty their pockets.

Messenger   Please sir . . .

Gryce   Quiet lad and get your pockets emptied.

(*He moves along the line inspecting the contents distastefully.*)

This can't be true, I don't believe it.

(*He puts the stick back on the desk.*)

Keep your hands out.

(*He goes along the line again frisking their clothing. He finally comes to the young boy.*)

Ah! Ah!

Messenger   Please sir . . .

Gryce   You're a regular little cigarette factory aren't you?

(He methodically takes the objects from the boy's pockets.)

You deceitful boy. You didn't think you could get away with a weak trick like that, did you?

(He puts all the objects into the basket.)

Right, one at a time, over here.

The three smokers, Billy, MacDowall and the boy individually come to the headmaster's desk, lean over it and are given two strokes each. It is important that this is done as realistically as possible and it should certainly not be funny in any way at all. The three smokers, Billy and MacDowall, although it hurts them, take it in their stride. As Gryce has already suggested, they will probably be back for more on another occasion. When it is the messenger's turn, however, Gryce has to direct him to the table and he leaves the room crying.

Scene 12

The English lesson.

Mr Farthing is giving books out to the class when Billy walks in.

Billy   I've just been to see Mr Gryce, sir.

Mr Farthing   Yes, I know. How many this time?

Billy   Two.

Mr Farthing   Sting?

Billy   Not bad.

Mr Farthing   Right, sit down then.

(Pause as Billy sits down.)

Right . . . Anderson. We've been talking about fact and fiction. I want you to stand up and tell us something about yourself – a fact – that is really interesting.

Anderson	I don't know anything sir.
Mr Farthing	Anything at all Anderson. Something that's happened to you, which sticks in your mind.

Anderson begins to smile.

Anderson	There's something but it's daft though.
Mr Farthing	Well, tell us then and let's all have a laugh.
Anderson	Well it was once when I was a kid. I was at junior school, I think, or somewhere like that, and went down to Fowlers Pond, me and this other kid. Reggie Clay they called him, he didn't come to this school; he flitted and went away somewhere. Anyway it was spring, tadpole time, and it's swarming with tadpoles down there in spring. Edges of the pond are all black with them, and me and this other kid started to catch them. It was easy, all you did, you just put your hands together and scooped a handful of water up and you'd got a handful of tadpoles. Anyway we were mucking about with them, picking them up and chucking them back and things, and we were on about taking some home, but we'd no jam jars. So this kid, Reggie, says, 'Take your Wellingtons off and put some in there, they'll be all right 'til you get home'. So I took them off and we put some water in them and then we started to put taddies in them. We kept ladling them in and I said to this kid, 'Let's have a competition, you have one Wellington and I'll have the other, and we'll see who can get most in'! So he started to fill one Wellington and I started to fill the other. We must have been at it hours, and they got thicker and thicker, until at the end there was no water left in them, they were just jam packed with tadpoles. You ought to have seen them, all black and shiny, right up to the top. When we'd finished we kept dipping our fingers into them and whipping them up at each other, all shouting and excited like. Then this kid said to me, 'I bet you daren't put one on'. And I said, 'I bet you daren't'. So we said we'd put one on each. We wouldn't though,

we kept reckoning to, then running away, so we tossed up and him who lost had to do it first. And I lost, oh, and you'd to take your socks off as well. So I took my socks off, and I kept looking at this Wellington full of tadpoles, and this kid kept saying, 'Go on then, you're frightened, you're frightened'. I was as well. Anyway I shut my eyes and started to put my foot in. OOoo, it was just like putting your feet into live jelly. They were frozen. And when my foot went down, they all came over the top of my Wellington and when I got my foot to the bottom, I could feel them all squashing about between my toes. Anyway, I'd done it, and I says to this kid, 'You put yours on now'. But he wouldn't, he was dead scared, so I put it on instead. I'd got used to it then, it was all right after a bit; it sent your legs all excited and tingling like. When I'd got them both on I started to walk up to this kid, waving my arms and making spook noises; and as I walked they all came squelching over the tops again and ran down the sides. This kid looked frightened to death, he kept looking down at my Wellingtons so I tried to run at him and they all spurted up my legs. You ought to have seen him. He just screamed out and ran home roaring. It was a funny feeling though when he'd gone; all quiet, with nobody there, and up to the knees in tadpoles.

Mr Farthing Very good Anderson. Thank you. Now has anyone else got anything interesting to tell us all?

(*No hands go up. Billy is fidgeting on his chair after receiving the cane.*)

What about you Casper?

(*Billy does not hear him.*)

Casper!

Billy What sir?

Mr Farthing Have you been listening?

Billy Yes sir.

Mr Farthing	Then tell us what we've been talking about.
Billy	Er . . . stories sir.
Mr Farthing	What kind of stories?
Billy	Er . . .
Mr Farthing	You don't know, do you?
Tibbut	He's been asleep again sir.
Billy	Shut your gob Tibbut.
Mr Farthing	Casper. Tibbut. You'll both be asleep in a minute. I'll knock you to sleep.
	(*Class are quiet.*)
	Right Casper you can do the work for a change. You're going to tell us a story – just like Anderson – any story at all, about yourself. Stand up.
Billy	I don't know any sir.
Mr Farthing	I'm giving you two minutes to think of something lad, and if you haven't started then the whole class is coming back at four.
	(*Immediate reaction from the class. Various pupils shout out.*)
Holmes	Come on Billy.
Cartledge	Or else you die!
Baker	Say anything.
Barr	If I've to come back I'll kill him.
Mr Farthing	I'm waiting Casper.
	(*Pause*)
Baker	Tell him about your hawk Casper.
Mr Farthing	If anyone else calls out it will be the last call he'll make . . . What hawk Casper? . . . It is a stuffed one?
	(*The whole class laugh. Billy is upset and he wipes his eyes.*)
	What's so funny about that? Well Tibbut?
Tibbut	He's got a hawk sir, it's a kestrel. He's mad about it. He never comes out with anybody else now, he just looks after this hawk. He's crackers with it.

Billy	It's better than you any day Tibbut.
	Mr Farthing sits down. Pause.
Mr Farthing	Now then Billy, come on, tell me about this hawk . . . where did you get it from?
	Billy is looking down at his desk.
Billy	Found it.
Mr Farthing	Where?
Billy	In a wood.
Mr Farthing	What had happened to it; was it injured?
Billy	It was a young one. It must have tumbled from a nest.
Mr Farthing	And where do you keep it?
Billy	In our shed.
Mr Farthing	Isn't that cruel?
	Billy looks at him for the first time.
Billy	I don't keep it in the shed all the time. I fly it every day.
Mr Farthing	And doesn't it fly away? I thought hawks were wild.
Billy	'Course it doesn't fly away. I've trained it.
Mr Farthing	Was it difficult?
Billy	'Course it was. You've to be right . . . right patient with them and take your time.
Mr Farthing	Come out here then and tell us all about it.
	(*Billy goes out hesitatingly.*)
	Right, how did you set about training it?
Billy	I started training Kes when I'd had her about a fortnight. She was as fat as a pig though at first. You can't do much with them until you've got their weight down. Gradually you cut their food down, until you go in one time and they're keen. I could tell with Kes because she jumped straight on my glove as I held it towards her. So while she was feeding I got hold of her jesses.
Mr Farthing	Her what?

Billy	Jesses. She wears them on her legs all the time so you can get hold of them as she sits on your glove.
Mr Farthing	And how do you spell that?
Billy	J–E–S–S–E–S.
Mr Farthing	Right, tell us more.
Billy	Then when she's on your glove you get the swivel – like a swivel on a dog lead – then you thread your leash – that's a leather thong – through your swivel, do you see?
Mr Farthing	Yes, I see. Carry on.
Billy	So you wrap your leash round your fingers so Kes is now fastened to your hand. When you've reached this stage and she's feeding from your hand regular and not bating too much . . .
Mr Farthing	Bating . . . what's that?
Billy	Trying to fly off, in a panic like. So now you can try feeding her outside and getting her used to things.

(Billy is now becoming more confident in telling his story.)

But you start inside first, making her jump on to your glove for the meat. Every time she comes you give her a scrap of meat. A reward like. Then when she'll come about a leash length straight away you can try her outside, off a fence or something. You put her down, hold on to the end of the leash with your right hand and hold your glove out for her to fly to.

(Billy is now doing the basic mime actions to accompany the story.)

When she's done this a bit you attach a creance instead of a leash – that's a long line, I used a fishing line. Then you put the hawk down on the fence post. Then you walk into the middle of the field unwinding the creance and the hawk's waiting for you to stop and hold your glove up. It's so it can't fly away you see.

Mr Farthing	It sounds very skilful and complicated Billy.
Billy	It doesn't sound half as bad as it is though. I've told you in a couple of minutes but it takes weeks to do all that. They're as stubborn as mules, hawks. Sometimes she'd be all right, then next time I'd go in the shed and she'd go mad, screaming and bating as though she'd never seen me before. You'd think that you'd learnt her something, you'd put her away feeling champion and then the next time you went you were back where you started.
Mr Farthing	You make it sound very exciting though.
Billy	It is, but the most exciting thing was when I flew her free for the first time. You ought to have been there then. I was frightened to death.

(*Mr Farthing turns to the class:*)

Mr Farthing	Do you want to hear about it?
Class	Yes sir.
Mr Farthing	Carry on Casper.
Billy	Well, I'd been flying her on the creance for about a week and she was coming to me anything up to thirty, forty yards. It says in the book that when it's coming this far, straight away, it's ready to fly loose. I daren't though. I kept saying to myself. I'll just use the creance today to make sure, then I'll fly it free tomorrow. I did this for about four days and I got right mad with myself. So on the last day I didn't feed her up, just to make sure that she'd be sharp set the next morning. I hardly went to sleep that night, I was thinking about it that much. When I got up next morning – it was a Saturday – I thought right, if she flies off, she flies off and it can't be helped. So I went down to the shed. She was dead keen as well, walking about on her shelf behind the bars and screaming out when she saw me coming. So I took her out on the field and tried her on the creance first time and she came like a rocket. So I thought right, this time. I unclipped the creance and

let her hop on to the fence post. There was nothing stopping her now. She could have flown off and there was nothing I could have done about it. I was terrified. I thought, she's forced to go, she's forced to go. She'll just fly off and that will be it. But she didn't. She just sat there looking round while I backed off into the field. I went right into the middle. Then I held my glove up and shouted her.

(*He is miming the action.*)

Come on Kes, come on then. Nothing happened at first. Then just as I was going to walk back to her, she came. Straight as a die, about a yard off the floor. She came twice as fast as when she had the creance on. She came like lightning, head dead still and her wings never made a sound. Then wham! Straight on to the glove, claws out grabbing for the meat. I was that pleased I didn't know what to do with myself, so I thought, just to prove it, I'll try her again, and she came the second time just as good. Well that was it. I'd trained her. I'd done it.

Mr Farthing   Right, that was very good. I enjoyed that and I'm sure the class did as well.

Splatter of applause from the class, Billy sits down.

Scene 13

Breaktime.

Billy is standing alone in one part of the playground. Groups of boys are standing around talking, playing about, etc. One such group includes MacDowall who sees Billy across the playground.

MacDowall   What's up Casper, don't you like company? They say your mother does. I hear you've got more uncles than any kid in this city.

Billy   Shut your mouth. Shut it can't you?

MacDowall   Come and make me.

Billy	You can only pick on little kids. You daren't pick on anybody your own size.
MacDowall	Who daren't?
Billy	You. You wouldn't say what you've just said to our Jud.
MacDowall	I'm not frightened of him. He's nothing your Jud. He wouldn't stick up for you anyway. He isn't even your brother.
Billy	What is he then, my sister?
MacDowall	He's not your right brother, my mother says. They don't call him Casper for a start.
Billy	'Course he's my brother. We live in the same house don't we?
MacDowall	You're nothing like brothers.
Billy	I'm tellin' him! I'm tellin' him what you say MacDowall.
	Billy rushes at him but MacDowall merely pushes him away without difficulty.
MacDowall	Get away you squirt, before I spit on you and drown you.
	Billy rushes at him again and they begin to fight. All the other groups of boys circle round them shouting. Before long Mr Farthing enters and pushes his way through to the centre of the group. They stop fighting and the crowd settle down a little.
Mr Farthing	I'm giving you lot ten seconds to get back to the yard. If I see one face after that time, I'll give its owner the biggest beating he's ever had.
	(They go off, some a little slower than others.)
	Now then, what's going off? Well . . . Casper?
Billy	It was his fault.
MacDowall	It was him.
Mr Farthing	All right. It's the same old story – nobody's fault. I ought to send both of you to Mr Gryce. Look at the mess you've made.

(*Billy is wiping his eyes.*)

And stop blubbering Casper, you're not dead yet.

MacDowall He will be when I get hold of him.

(*Mr Farthing goes up to MacDowall.*)

Mr Farthing You're a brave boy aren't you MacDowall. If you're so keen on fighting why don't you pick on somebody your own size?

(*Mr Farthing starts poking him.*)

Because you're scared aren't you MacDowall? You're nothing but a bully, the classic example of a bully. What would you say if I pinned you to the floor and smacked you across the face?

(*He begins prodding him harder.*)

MacDowall I'll tell my dad.

Mr Farthing Of course you will lad. Boys like you always tell their dads. And then do you know what I'll do MacDowall? I'll tell mine.

(*He begins to shout.*)

So what's going to happen to your dad then? Eh? And what's going to happen to you? Eh? Eh MacDowall?

(*He lets MacDowall go.*)

Right, get back into school, get cleaned up and get to your lesson. And let that be the last time that you even think about bullying. Understand?

MacDowall Yes sir.

(*He goes.*)

Mr Farthing Now then, Casper, what's it all about?

Billy I can't tell you right sir.

Mr Farthing Why can't you?

(*Pause*)

Billy Well . . . he started calling me names and saying things about my mother and our Jud and everybody was laughing and . . .

(He starts crying.)

Mr Farthing All right lad, calm down. It's finished with now. I don't know, you always seem to be in trouble. I wonder why. Why do you think it is?

Billy Because everybody picks on me, that's why.

Mr Farthing Perhaps it's because you're a bad lad.

Billy Perhaps I am sometimes. But I'm no worse than lots of kids and they seem to get away with it.

Mr Farthing You think you're just unlucky then?

Billy I don't know sir. I seem to get into bother for daft things. Like this morning in the hall. I wasn't doing anything. I just dozed off. I'd been up since seven, then I had to run round with the papers, then run home to have a look at the hawk, then run to school. You'd have been tired if you'd done that sir.

Mr Farthing I'd have been exhausted.

Billy It's nothing to get the stick for though sir. You can't tell Gryce – Mr Gryce – though, or he'd kill you. And this morning in English when I wasn't listening. It wasn't that I wasn't bothered, it was my backside, it was killing me. You can't concentrate when your backside's stinging like mad.

Mr Farthing No, I don't suppose you can.

Billy Teachers never think it might be their fault either.

Mr Farthing No, I don't think many do lad.

Billy Like when you get thumped for not listening when it's dead boring. You can't help not listening when it's not interesting. Can you sir?

Mr Farthing No you can't Casper.

(Pause. Billy looks down and starts playing with his hands.)

How are things at home these days?

Billy All right, same as usual I suppose.

Mr Farthing What about the police? Been in any trouble lately?

Billy No sir.

Mr Farthing	Reformed or not been caught?
Billy	Reformed sir. There's always somebody after me though. If anything goes wrong on the estate, police always come to our house, even though I've done nothing for ages now.
Mr Farthing	Never mind lad, it'll be all right.
Billy	Yes it will that.
Mr Farthing	Just think, you'll be leaving school in a few weeks, starting your first job, meeting fresh people. That's something to look forward to isn't it?
	(*Billy hunches his shoulders and doesn't answer.*)
	Have you got a job yet?
Billy	No sir. I've to see the Youth Employment bloke this afternoon.
Mr Farthing	What kind of job are you after?
Billy	I shan't have much choice, shall I? I shall have to take what they've got.
Mr Farthing	I thought you'd have been looking forward to leaving.
Billy	I'm not bothered.
Mr Farthing	I thought you didn't like school.
Billy	I don't but that don't mean that I'll like work does it? Still, I'll get paid for not liking it, that's one thing.
Mr Farthing	Yes. Well I'll have to blow the whistle.
	(*Billy begins to leave.*)
	Oh Casper.
Billy	What sir?
Mr Farthing	This hawk of yours. I'd like to see it sometime.
Billy	Yes sir.
Mr Farthing	When do you fly it?
Billy	Dinner times. Gets dark too early at nights.
Mr Farthing	Do you fly it at home?
Billy	Yes.
Mr Farthing	Woods Avenue, isn't it?

Billy Yes sir, 124.

Mr Farthing Good, I'll be down then sometime if that's O.K.

Billy 'Course.

(*Whistle blows.*)

End of Act One

ACT TWO

Scene 14

The P.E. changing room.

Before the scene begins properly the P.E. class enter walking casually. They are talking among themselves in the normal way. Martin and Allen are standing at the front of the group talking.

Martin I hate P.E. with him. It's always football. This weather as well.

Allen We haven't been in the Gym for years now.

Martin Other classes do basketball sometimes.

Allen Where is he anyway? Is he here today?

Martin Oh he'll be here all right. He wouldn't miss double football for anything.

Sugden runs into the changing room and twice round it.

Sugden Right lads. No time for shirking. Let's have you changed. Changed and out. You should be pushing at the door fully kitted up shouting, 'Let's get out sir, to the field, to the field'.

(Billy enters.)

Skyving again Casper?

Billy No sir, Mr Farthing wanted me – he's been talking to me.

Sugden I bet that was stimulating for him, wasn't it?

Billy What does that mean sir?

Sugden The conversation, lad, what do you think it means?

Billy No sir, that word, stimu . . . stimu . . . la . . . tin.

Sugden Stimulating you fool–S–T–I–M–U–L–A–T–I–N–G stimulating.

35

Billy	Yes sir.
Sugden	Well get changed lad – You're two weeks late already.
	(*Looks at watch.*)
	Some of us want a game even if you don't.
Billy	I've no kit sir.
	(*Pause*)
Sugden	Casper. You make me sick. Every lesson it's the same old story. 'Please Sir, I've got no kit.' Every lesson for five years! And in all that time you've made no attempt whatsoever to get any kit. You've skyved and scrounged and borrowed and . . . Why is that everyone else can get some, but you can't?
Billy	I don't know sir. My mother won't buy me any. She says it's a waste of money, especially now that I'm leaving.
Sugden	You've not been leaving for five years have you?
Billy	No sir.
Sugden	You could have bought some out of your spending money, couldn't you?
Billy	I don't like football sir.
Sugden	What's that got to do with it?
Billy	I don't know sir. Anyway I don't get enough.
Sugden	You should get a job then, I don't . . .
Billy	I've got one sir.
Sugden	Well then, you get paid don't you?
Billy	Yes sir, but I've to give it to my mam. I'm still paying her for my fines, like instalments every week.
	Sugden bounces the ball on his head.
Sugden	Well you should keep out of trouble then lad, and then . . .
Billy	I've not been in trouble sir, not . . .

Sugden   Shut up lad! Shut up, before you drive me crackers.

(He hits him with the ball twice. He goes into his room and brings out a giant pair of drawers.)

Here Casper, get them on.

(He throws them at Billy.)

Billy   They'll not fit me sir.

(The class laugh.)

Sugden   What are you talking about lad? You can get them on, can't you?

Billy   Yes sir.

Sugden   Well they fit you then. Now get changed. Quick.

Billy gets changed into the shorts.

Sugden   You, Palmer, come here lad.

Palmer   What sir?

Sugden   Ten press-ups. Come on. With me.

Palmer   I can't do press-ups sir.

Sugden   No I don't suppose you can. Get down.

They both begin doing press-ups as everyone continues getting changed. After three, Sugden begins to tire and he only just manages four. The boy is still going strong. Sugden stops.

(Sugden is panting.)

Sugden   Yes, well . . . er . . . that's enough lad. You don't want to injure yourself.

The class laugh out loud at Billy who has now got his 'shorts' on. The tops of them are up to his chest, and the bottoms below his knees.

Sugden   Roll them down and don't be so foolish. You're too daft to laugh at Casper. Right get lined up. Let's get two sides picked. Tibbut, come out here and be the other captain.

(Billy jumps to keep warm.)

Stop prancing Casper, are you mad?

Billy   I'm frozen sir. I'm just jumping to keep warm.

Sugden   Well don't lad. I'll have first pick Tibbut.

Tibbut   That's not right sir.

Sugden   Why isn't it right?

Tibbut   'Cos you'll get all the best players.

Sugden   Rubbish lad.

Tibbut   'Course you will sir, it's not fair.

Sugden   Tibbut. Do you want to play football or do you want to get dressed and do maths?

Tibbut   Football sir.

Sugden   Right then, stop moaning and start picking. I'll have . . .

(Sugden and Tibbut use the real names of the characters or make them up and two sides are picked. Sugden takes a coin from his tracksuit bottoms and tosses it.)

Sugden   Call Tibbut.

Tibbut   Tails.

Sugden   It's heads. We'll play downhill. Are we all ready to go? Casper. What position are you?

Billy   Don't know sir – I've not decided yet.

Sugden   Goal, Casper. You'll go in goal, you're no good out.

Billy   Oh sir, I can't goal, I'm no good.

Sugden   Now's your chance to learn then isn't it?

Billy   I'm fed up of going in goal. I go in every week. Don't blame me when i let 'em all through.

Sugden   Of course I'll blame you lad! Who do you expect me to blame?

Tibbut   Who are you today sir, Liverpool?

Sugden   Rubbish lad, don't you know your club colours yet?

Tibbut   Liverpool are red aren't they sir?

Sugden   Yes, but they're all red, shirts, shorts and stockings. These are Manchester United's colours.

Tibbut	'Course they are sir, I forgot. What position are you playing?
	Sugden turns round to reveal a No. 9 on his back.
Sugden	Bobby Charlton.
Tibbut	Bobby Charlton? I thought you were usually Dennis Law when you were Manchester United?
Sugden	It's too cold to play as a striker today. I'm scheming this morning, all over the field, just like Charlton used to do.
Tibbut	Law played all over sir. He wasn't just a striker.
Sugden	He didn't link like Charlton.
Tibbut	Better player though sir.
Sugden	Are you trying to tell me about football Tibbut?
Tibbut	No sir.
Sugden	Well shut up then. Anyway Law's in the wash this week.
Martin	Let's go sir. It's getting cold standing here.
	(Sugden points to Martin.)
Sugden	Watch it lad! Right get lined up.
	(Sugden now imitates a television football commentator.)
	. . . And both teams are now lined up ready to come out for this vital fifth round cup tie, Manchester United versus . . . Who are we playing Tibbut?
	Tibbut looks round at the team lined up behind him dressed in multi-coloured kit.
Tibbut	Er . . . We'll be Liverpool sir.
Sugden	You can't be Liverpool lad, there'll be a clash of colours.
	He looks again.
Tibbut	Er . . . we'll be Spurs then sir, then there'll be no clash of colours.
Sugden	. . . And it's Manchester United versus Spurs in this vital fifth round cup tie. And the teams are ready.

And I think that they're about to come out. Yes here they come. The teams are coming out. I can see them. They're here. They're here. Just listen to that roar.

Scene 15

Billy's house.

Billy comes into the house and has a drink of milk from the bottle on the table. He sees two 10p pieces and a betting slip that Jud has left for him to take to the bookmakers. He reads it slowly.

Billy 20p Double 'Crackpot', 'Tell him he's dead'. Jud. Bloody hell.

(*He picks up the money.*)

Heads I take it. Tails I don't.

(*Tosses coin.*)

Heads . . . best out of three.

(*Tosses again.*)

Tails.

(*He grins slightly to himself. Tosses again.*)

Heads . . . shit.

He folds the slip of paper and puts it and the money in his pocket. He goes to the hut to see Kes before going to the bookmakers.

Scene 16

Kes's hut.

Billy is about to go after checking that Kes is all right when Mr Farthing approaches.

Mr Farthing Casper.

(*Billy speaks quietly.*)

Billy	Bloody hell fire.
Mr Farthing	Can I have a look?
Billy	'Course. Not too close though sir, she's nervous today. Don't know why.
Mr Farthing	Beautiful isn't it? Do you know, this is the first time I've really been close to a hawk.

(He touches the door of the hut but snatches his hand back.)

Goodness, not very friendly. Seems all right with you though.

Billy	Only because I'm not bothered though.
Mr Farthing	How do you mean?
Billy	Well when she used to peck me – when I first had her – I kept my finger there as though it didn't hurt. So after a bit she packed it in.
Mr Farthing	I'd never have thought of that.

(Pause)

You think a lot about that bird don't you?

Billy	'Course I do. Wouldn't you if it was yours? I had a little fox cub once, reared it and let it go. It was a little blinder. I've kept loads of birds as well.
Mr Farthing	Which was your favourite?

Billy stares at him, surprised that he has asked such a question.

Billy	You what sir?
Mr Farthing	You mean the hawk?
Billy	The others weren't in the same class.
Mr Farthing	What's so special about this one then?

(Pause)

Billy	I don't know right. It just is that's all.
Mr Farthing	What I like about it is its shape. It's so beautifully proportioned. The neat head. The way the wings fold over the back. And that down on its thighs – just like plus-fours.

Billy It's when it's flying though, sir, that's when it's got it over other birds; that's when it's at its best.

(Pause)

Do you know sir, I feel as though she's doing me a favour just letting me stand here and look at her.

Mr Farthing It's proud of itself. It demands respect from you.

Billy That's why it makes me mad when I take her out and somebody says, 'Look at Billy Casper with his pet hawk'. I could shout at them. It's not a pet, sir, hawks are not pets. It's not tame, it's trained that's all. It's fierce and it's wild and it's not bothered about anybody. Not even me right. And that's why it's great.

Mr Farthing A lot of people wouldn't understand that though. They like pets they can make friends with; make a fuss of, cuddle a bit, boss a bit. Don't you agree?

Billy Yes, I suppose so, but I'm not bothered about that though. I'd sooner have her just to look at her and fly her. That's enough for me. They can keep their rabbits and their budgies, they're rubbish compared with her.

Mr Farthing Yes, I think you're right. It's difficult when you try to think why though. It's not its size is it? It doesn't look particularly fearsome either; in fact it sometimes looks positively babyish.

Billy Yes sir.

Mr Farthing I think it's a kind of pride, a kind of independence. It seems to have a satisfaction with its own beauty. It seems to look you in the eye and say, 'who are you anyway?'

(Pause. Then he looks at his watch.)

Good lord! Look at the time. We'd better be off. I'll give you a lift if you like.

Billy It's all right sir.

Mr Farthing What's the matter, would your reputation suffer if you were seen travelling with a teacher?

Billy	It's not that. I've got one or two things to do first.
Mr Farthing	Right. I'll be off then. Don't be late. And thanks a lot, I enjoyed that.

They go off in different directions.

Scene 17

Bookmaker's shop.

People are sitting around on chairs, some looking at newspapers, some waiting for the next race to begin. Mrs Rose is taking bets behind the counter. Billy enters.

Mrs Rose	Can I help you, lad?
Billy	No it's all right.

He looks round, sees a space on a bench next to one of the men reading a newspaper and sits down. After a short time Billy speaks, holding out Jud's betting slip:

Billy	I say mister, what price are these two?
Man	What are they?

(He takes the betting slip.)

'Crackpot' ... 100–6, And 'Tell him he's dead', that's ... where is it? I've just been looking at that myself. 'Tell ... him ... he's ... dead', here it is ...4–1 favourite.

(Gives the slip back to Billy.)

100–6 and 4–1.

Pause. Billy looks down at the slip.

Billy	Have they got a chance?
Man	Now then lad, how do I know?
Billy	Would you back them?

(The man consults the newspaper again.)

Man	'Tell him he's dead' has got a good chance. It's top weight. It's the best horse in the race. It must be or it

wouldn't be the top weight would it? I don't fancy the other though. No form. Not even a jockey on it in here. It'll have a lad on it you can bet. No I wouldn't bother with that one.

Billy   You don't think they'll win then?

Man   How've you got them – doubled?

Billy   They're not mine, they're our Jud's.

Man   He'll be all right if they do – I can't see it myself though.

Billy stands up, walks round a little thinking what to do. He finally screws up the betting slip, drops it in the bin and goes out.

Billy   Thanks mister.

Scene 18

The butcher's shop.

Mr Beal, the butcher, is cutting meat on the counter as Billy enters eating chips.

Billy   Quarter of beef.

Mr Beal   My, them smell good.

Billy   Do you want one?

Mr Beal takes a few.

Mr Beal   Lovely. Got them from Mrs Hartley's have you?

Billy   That's right.

Mr Beal   Makes good chips does Mrs Hartley.

(Billy continues eating the chips as Mr Beal begins to get the meat for him.)

Quarter of beef you say?

Billy   Yes.

Mr Beal   You've still got that bird then?

Billy   Yes.

Mr Beal wraps the meat up.

Mr Beal Here, you can have that.

Billy For nothing?

Mr Beal They're only scraps.

Billy Thanks. Do you want another chip?

Mr Beal No, I'll be going for my dinner in a bit.

Billy Cheerio, then.

Mr Beal So long.

Scene 19

A school corridor.

Two boys, Delamore and Gibbs, are standing discussing what lessons they are supposed to go to next. Jud enters the school, very annoyed.

Jud Have you seen our Billy?

Delamore Billy who?

Jud Casper.

Delamore No, not lately.

Gibbs I haven't either.

Jud Do you know him?

Delamore 'Course I know him.

Gibbs 'Course we know him.

Jud Do you think you will see him?

Delamore Don't know, might do might not.

Gibbs Just depends.

Jud If you do, tell him you've seen me.

Delamore What do you want him for anyway?

Jud He should have put a bet on for me but he didn't. He kept the money.

Jud goes off. Delamore and Gibbs are about to do the same when they see Billy.

Gibbs	Hey, Casper, have you seen your Jud yet?
Billy	No – why?
Delamore	He wants you, he's in school somewhere.
Billy	What for?
Gibbs	He's been hanging around a bit now. He's just been here looking for you.
Billy	What for though?
Delamore	I don't know. Something about a bet.
Billy	Christ. How long ago?
Gibbs	'Couple of minutes. We were just coming out of French. He was waiting outside. He must have thought that you were in our class.
Delamore	I reckon he's going to thump you one. I should watch out.
Gibbs	He looked right mad.

Delamore and Gibbs go off as Palmer and Rogers enter.

Billy	I say, have you seen our Jud?
Palmer	Where've you been? They've been looking all over for you.
Billy	Who has?
Palmer	Gryce pudding and everybody.
Billy	What for – I haven't done anything.
Rogers	Youth Employment. You should have gone for your interview last lesson.
Billy	Have you seen our Jud though?
Rogers	Earlier on – over near the boiler room – why?
Billy	Did he say anything?
Palmer	He just asked where you were that's all. What you hiding from him for?
Billy	Have you seen him since?
Rogers	What's the matter – is he after you for something?

Gryce enters behind Billy. The other two see him and immediately go. Gryce hits Billy twice.

Gryce shouts:

Gryce And where do you think you've been lad?

Billy Nowhere sir.

Gryce Nowhere? Don't talk ridiculous lad. Who do you think you are – the invisible man?

Billy I felt sick sir – so I went to the lavatory.

Gryce And where were you – down it? I sent prefects to the toilets. They said you weren't there.

Billy I went outside then sir, for a breath of fresh air.

Gryce I'll give you fresh air.

Billy I've just come back in, sir.

Gryce And what about your interview? I've had the whole school out looking for you.

Billy I'm just going sir.

Gryce Well get off then. And God help anyone who employs you.

Billy Er . . . where to sir?

Gryce The medical room lad. If you'd stay awake in assembly you'd know where to.

(Billy exits quickly. Gryce also goes off but almost walks into a young pupil.)

Gryce Get over lad. Don't you know to keep to the right hand side yet?

Scene 20

The medical room

On one side of the stage the Youth Employment (Y.E.) Officer, a mother and her son are talking although they cannot be heard because they are 'inside' the room. On the other side of the stage are three chairs. Billy enters and sits on one of these. Before long he begins to fidget as he is impatient and also worried

about Jud being in school. He stands up, walks round
and sits down again. Allender and his mother enter
and sit on the other two chairs. Billy and Allender nod
to each other. Pause.

Mrs Allender And don't be sat there like a dummy when you get in. Tell him you're after a good job. An office job. Something like that.

Allender Who's after an office job?

Mrs Allender Well what are you after then? A job on the bins?

Allender I wish you'd shut up.

Mrs Allender Straighten your tie.

Allender I wish you'd stop nagging.

Mrs Allender Somebody's got to nag.

Allender I wish you'd go home.

Billy Is it your mam?

The mother and son 'inside' the office shake hands
with the Youth Employment Officer and leave. The two
mothers smile at each other and pass comments on
the weather.

Y. E. Officer Next.

(Billy looks round and then goes in.)

Well come in lad if you're coming. I haven't got all day. Sit down Walker.

Billy I'm not Walker.

Y. E. Officer Well who are you then? According to my list it should be Gerald Walker next.
(He checks his list.)

Oliver, Stenton, then Walker.

Billy I'm Casper.

Y. E. Officer Casper? . . . Casper? Oh yes, I should have seen you earlier shouldn't I.

(He finds Billy's card.)

Casper . . . Casper. Here we are. Mmmm. Now then Casper, what kind of job have you in mind?

(*Pause*)

Well?

Billy Don't know. Haven't thought about it right.

Y. E. Officer Well, you should be thinking about it. You want to start off on the right foot don't you?

Billy I suppose so.

Y. E. Officer You haven't looked around for anything yet then?

Billy No, not yet.

Y. E. Officer Right then. Would you like to work in an office? Or would you prefer manual work?

Billy What's that . . . manual work?

Y. E. Officer It means working with your hands, for example, building, farming, engineering. Jobs like that, as opposed to pen-pushing jobs.

Billy I'd be all right working in an office, wouldn't I? I've a job to read and write.

Y. E. Officer Have you thought about entering a trade as an apprentice? You know, as an electrician, or a bricklayer or something like that. Of course the money isn't too good while you're serving your apprenticeship. You may find that lads of your own age who take dead end jobs will be earning far more than you; but in those jobs there's no satisfaction or security and if you do stick it out, you'll find it well worth your while. Well what do you think about it?

(*No reaction from Billy.*)

As you've already said you feel better working with your hands, perhaps this would be your best bet. Of course, it would mean attending Technical College and studying for various examinations but nowadays most employers encourage their lads to take advantage of these facilities and allow them time off to attend – usually one day a week.

(He gets up from his chair, looks out of the window and continues talking.)

On the other hand, if your firm wouldn't allow you time off during the day, and you were still keen to study, then you'd have to attend classes in your own time. Some lads do it for years – two or three nights a week from leaving school until their middle twenties, when some take their Higher National or even degrees.

(He turns round.)

Had you considered continuing your education in any form after leaving school?

(No reaction from Billy.)

I say, are you listening lad?

Billy   Yes.

Y. E. Officer   You don't look as though you are to me. I

haven't got all day you know, I've other lads to see before four o'clock. Now then, where were we? If nothing I've mentioned already appeals to you, and if you can stand a hard day's graft and not mind getting dirty, then there are good opportunities in mining.

Billy   I'm not going down the pit.

Y. E. Officer   Conditions have improved tremendously . . .

Billy   I wouldn't be seen dead down the pit.

Y. E. Officer   Well, what do you want to do then? There

doesn't seem to be a job in England to suit you.

(Pause)

What about hobbies. What hobbies have you got? What about gardening or constructing Meccano sets or anything like that?

(Billy slowly shakes his head.)

No hobbies at all?

(Billy stands up.)

Billy   Can I go now?

Y. E. Officer   What's the matter lad? Sit down. I haven't
finished yet.

(*The Youth Employment Officer takes a form and
begins to fill it in.*)

Well, I've interviewed some lads in my time, but I've
never met one like you. Half the time you're like a
cat on hot bricks – the other half you're not
listening.

(*He picks up a booklet.*)

Here, take this home and read it. It gives you all the
relevant information concerned with leaving school
and starting work. Things like sickness benefits,
national insurance, pensions, etc.

(*Billy is not listening at all by this time and very
anxious to get out of the room.*)

At the back there's a detachable form. When you
want your cards fill it in and send it to the office. The
address is at the top. Have you got that?

(*Billy nods.*)

Well, take it then . . . and if you have any trouble
getting fixed up come in and see me. O.K.? Right
Casper, that's all. Tell the next boy to come in.

*Billy hurries out leaving the Youth Employment Officer
slowly shaking his head.*

Scene 21

Billy's house.
Billy is heard shouting before he enters.

Billy   Kes!

He runs over to Kes's hut, but the door to it is open.
Kes!

He hurries into the kitchen.

Jud . . . Jud! Mother!

He goes back towards the hut.

Kes! Jud!

He runs off.

Kes! Kes!

Scene 22

The high street.

Mrs Rose from the bookmaker's enters. Billy runs up to her.

Billy Hey, Mrs Rose.

(*He pauses for breath.*)

Have you seen our Jud?

Mrs Rose I can see that you haven't or else you wouldn't be in one piece now.

Billy You've seen him then?

Mrs Rose Seen him? He nearly ripped the place apart, that's all.

Billy Have you seen him since?

Mrs Rose He called me all the names under the sun. He said I was trying to rob his eyes out. Then he threatened Tommy Leach with violence when he tried to put a word in so Tommy walked out of the shop. 'You do right', I said to Tommy. A right pantomime. I had to send for Eric Clough and Eric Street in the end to prove that you never placed that bet.

Billy Has he been back?

Mrs Rose They both won, you know. 'Crackpot' got 100–8, 'Tell him he's dead' got 4–1. He'd have had £13 to draw.

Billy Do you know where he is now?

Mrs Rose Why didn't you put it on?

Billy begins to cry.

Billy	How do I know? I didn't know they were going to win did I?
Mrs Rose	You won't half get into trouble lad, when he gets hold of you.

Billy runs off.

Scene 23

Billy's house.

Mrs Casper and Jud are casually eating tea and reading a newspaper and a magazine.

Billy enters. It has been raining and he is wet.

Billy	Where is it? What have you done with it?
Mrs Casper	And where do you think you've been all this time? You're sodden. Get some tea.

(She goes back to her magazine.)

And shut that door Billy. There's a terrible draught behind you.

Billy shouts.

Billy	I said where is it?

Jud shouts back at him.

Jud	What are you staring at?
Mrs Casper	What's going off? What's all this bloody shouting about?
Billy	Ask him. He knows what it's about.

Jud gets up from the table.

Jud	Yes lad, and you'd have known if I'd have got hold of you earlier.
Mrs Casper	Known what? What are you both talking about?

(Billy begins to cry.)

Now then, what's the matter with you? What have you done to him now Jud?

Jud	It's his fault. If he'd have put that bet on like he was told, there would have been none of this.
Mrs Casper	Didn't he? Well I told him before I went to work this morning.
Jud	Did he, bloody hell.
Mrs Casper	I told you not to forget Billy.
Jud	He didn't forget – he kept the money.
Mrs Casper	And what happened? Did they win?
Jud	Win? I'd have had £13 to draw if he'd kept his thieving hands to himself.
Mrs Casper	£13. Billy, you've done it once too often this time.
Jud	£13. I could have had a few days off work with that. I'd have bloody killed him if I'd have got hold of him this afternoon.
Mrs Casper	What's he crying about then?
Billy	Because he's killed my hawk instead, that's why.
Mrs Casper	You haven't, have you Jud?
Billy	He has. I know he has. Just because he couldn't catch me.
Mrs Casper	Have you Jud?
Jud	All right then. So I've killed it. What are you going to do about it?
Billy	Mother!
	(*Billy rushes to his mother and tries to bury his face in her but she pushes him away, embarrassed.*)
Mrs Casper	Give over then Billy. Don't be so daft.
Jud	It was its own stupid fault. I was only going to let it go but it wouldn't get out of the hut. Every time I tried to shift it, it kept lashing out at my hands with its claws. Look at them, they're scratched to ribbons.
Billy	You bastard. You big rotten bastard.
Jud	Don't call me a bastard or you'll be the next to get it.
Billy	You bastard.

Mrs Casper	Shut up Billy. I'm not having that language in here.
Billy	Well do something then. Do something to him.
Mrs Casper	Where is it Jud? What have you done with it?

Jud turns away from the table.

Jud	It's in the bin.

Billy runs out to two dustbins near Kes's hut. He pushes the lid off the first but there is nothing there. He does the same to the second, and among the rubbish finds Kes, dead. He looks down on it for a few seconds, leaves it there and returns to the house. Mrs Casper and Jud have continued with their tea.

Billy	Have you seen what he's done Mam? Have you seen it?
Mrs Casper	I know love. It's a shame. But it can't be helped.
Billy	Come and look at it though. Look what he's done.
Mrs Casper	It were a rotten trick Jud.
Jud	It were a rotten trick what he did wasn't it?
Mrs Casper	I know but you know how much he thought of that bird.
Jud	He didn't think half as much of it as I did that 13 quid.
Mrs Casper	I know, but it was a rotten trick all the same.
Billy	It's not fair on him Mam. It's not fair on him.
Mrs Casper	I know it's not but it's done now so there's nothing we can do about it is there?
Billy	What about him? What are you going to do to him? I want you to do something to him.
Mrs Casper	What can I do? Don't be silly.
Billy	Hit him. Give him some fist.
Jud	I'd like to see her.
Mrs Casper	Talk sense, Billy, how can I hit him?
Billy	You never do anything to him. He gets away with everything.

Mrs Casper	Oh shut up now then. You've cried long enough about it.
Billy	You're not bothered about anything you.
Mrs Casper	Of course I'm bothered. But it's only a bird. You can get another can't you?

Billy lunges at Jud and starts thumping him. Jud stands up and starts hitting him back.)

What are you doing? Billy stop it, stop it! Jud leave him alone! Stop it both of you!

She tries to come between them. Billy swings his fist at her. They back away and he runs out of the house.

Mrs Casper	Billy, come back here. Come back here you young bugger.
Billy	You'll not catch me; you'll never catch me.

Lights fade down. Billy walks on. He takes Kes from inside his jacket, kneels down and digs a hole with his hands. He places Kes in the hole and covers it with the soil. Fade to blackout.

End

QUESTIONS AND EXPLORATIONS

Keeping Track

Act One

Scenes 1– 4

1 'Just think, in a few weeks you'll be coming down there with me' Jud says to Billy. What does this tell you about what people expect in the community where they both live?

2 Make a list of the things Jud does in the first scene which show how he bullies Billy.

3 What do we learn from Mr Porter about the estate where Billy lives?

4 Do you think that Mr Porter and the milkman have different opinions of Billy?

5 Mrs Casper is Billy's mother – what do we learn about her in this scene?

6 In these four scenes, we see Billy with four different people. He acts differently towards each one. Why do you think this is?

Scenes 5–9

1 In Scene 5 Billy first throws stones at MacDowall's window and later he throws dirt at the window. Why does Billy do this? What is the difference in the two actions and what would be the difficulty if you were staging this scene?

2 When talking to the farmer Billy makes his longest speech

in the play so far – why do you think this is? What effect does it have on the scene?

3 Throughout this scene Billy and the farmer show different attitudes to the kestrel. How are they similar and how are they different? Do each of them always tell the truth?

4 What evidence is there in Scene 7 that Billy has never been to a library before?

5 The librarian has to write a short official report about the loss of the book – how would she report what happened that afternoon?

6 Why does Billy steal the book?

7 Mrs Casper asks Billy about his book – what do we learn about her in the way she listens to the answers?

8 In Scene 9 why does Billy speak to Jud like this? Would he speak like this if Jud were sober?

9 Write a diary entry for Billy's Saturday.

10 Imagine you are Billy or Jud. Describe the bedroom or kitchen and include how you feel about it.

Scenes 10–13

1 In Scene 11 the headmaster talks about MacDowall, and MacDowall talks about the headmaster. What do we learn about each of them from the scene?

2 What are the main differences in the way that Mr Farthing and Mr Gryce speak to pupils?

3 Why do you think MacDowall picks on Billy?

4 Why does Billy fight with MacDowall at school but not with Jud at home?

Act Two

Scene 14

1 What is the purpose of this scene? Why has this scene been placed at the beginning of Act Two?

2 Would it have been possible to write this scene if it had been a girls' P.E. lesson?

Scenes 15–18

1 Why has Billy come home at lunchtime?

2 What is Billy's attitude towards Jud's bet? Where else has it been mentioned in the play? Why can't Jud place the bet himself?

3 What is so unusual about Mr Farthing's visit? Is it significant that 'Kes' is a she?

4 What similarities between Billy and the kestrel are highlighted in this scene?

5 What does Mr Farthing learn in this scene?

6 Why does Billy decide not to place the bet?

7 How does Billy spend Jud's money?

8 How long, in real time, elapses between the start of Scene 15 to the end of 18? Where does Billy spend most of his time? How is the pace of this section different from the other scenes around it?

Scenes 19–20

1 Who is looking for Billy? And why?

2 What is the difference between Mrs Allender and Mrs Casper?

3 Why is the Youth Employment Officer confused and irritated with Billy?

4 What is Billy's main concern in the scene with the Youth Employment Officer?

Scenes 21–23

1 Scene 21 is the shortest in the play. Why is it needed?

2 What is Mrs Rose's reaction to Billy?

3 How does Billy feel when he enters his house?

4 Why is Jud so annoyed?

5 How does Mrs Casper expect Billy to react to the death of Kes?

6 Why do they fight at the end of the play?

7 What is the significance of the final line of the play?

Explorations

A   Characters

1 Write a reference which Mr Porter would write for Billy. Begin:

To whom it may concern.
Billy Casper has worked for me for …

2 One person take on the character of Mr Porter and/or the milkman. Others ask them questions and they answer as this character. Question them about Billy, the estate, themselves and what they would like to happen in their lives.

3 Write what you know about the characters of Jud, Billy and Mrs Casper. You may like to do this by first drawing a

silhouette of the character and writing notes around the picture. Keep this and add to it as you read or re-read the play.

4 Write a school report for Billy. You will need to use your imagination about some of the subjects, as well as the evidence you have from the play.

5 Write notes for the actor playing the role of Mr Sugden. What do you expect him to look like? How should he play the role? What use should he make of his voice and his actions?

6 Discuss the different mother/son relationships portrayed in the play. Write Billy's, MacDowall's, and Allender's views of their mothers and their mothers' views of them.

7 Mr Farthing calls the kestrel 'it' whilst Billy refers to the bird as 'she' – what do you think it tells the audience about both people?

8 Write the formal report by the Youth Employment Officer of the careers interview between himself and Casper.

9 Read carefully the interview between the Youth Employment Officer and Billy Casper. Do you think Billy had any chance of receiving help from him? Try to find points in the interview, if any, where Billy could change the direction of his future. In pairs, try out these changes and the way the scene changes as a result.

10 *Kes* is a play about a boy, not a bird. Yet the female kestrel plays a very important role. Perhaps her main purpose is to act as a symbol. Of what?

11 That Billy manages to control a bird of prey is in itself significant because in most other areas of his life Billy himself is the victim of people and circumstances that prey on him. Billy is similar to Kes in some ways and in

other ways the freedom and total self-sufficiency of the bird acts as a contrast to Billy's trapped and dependent life. Find moments from the play that illustrate these differences and similarities.

12 Billy can be described in many ways. To some he is weedy, crackers, the joker and thick – but at other times he is the expert, the survivor and a determined boy. Find examples in the play that best illustrate these characteristics.

13 Imagine that you are Billy and that you want to write a memorial for Kes. What would you say about her?

14 What happens to Billy after Kes's death? Improvise scenes that take place a day, a week and a year later.

B Themes

a) Bullying

1 Billy is bullied by many people in the play, including his family and school. What happens and what is the difference between the actions of the bullies? In your opinion who is the worst bully?

2 '... I continue using the cane, knowing full well that you'll be back time and time again ...'

Is there any point to the headmaster's use of the cane? What sort of punishments do you think might work as well or better?

3 In what way is MacDowall a typical bully? Do you think that Mr Farthing deals with this incident effectively?

4 Is Mr Sugden a bully, or just self-centred? Are all teachers like Mr Sugden to some extent? Are all adults?

5 In Scene 11 a young boy is caned by Mr Gryce for something he didn't do. Write a letter from the parent of the

young boy to Mr Gryce asking for an explanation.

6 Design a bullying-prevention programme for your school. Include long-term plans for raising awareness among students and staff and suggest long-term measures for getting rid of bullying altogether.

7 Mr Gryce canes pupils who misbehave. Do you think that this is a good approach or not? Find out all you can about the debate surrounding corporal punishment in this country. How far has the European Community influenced the debate?

8 As a group, conduct a survey of your parents to see where their sympathies lie on corporal punishment.

b) School

9 What similarities and differences are there between Billy's school and your own?

10 Talk to parents, teachers, or friends who have left school. What do they remember about their schooldays? Make notes about the changes.

11 *Kes* takes place in an all boys' school. How would it be different in a mixed school? What are the advantages and disadvantages of a mixed, comprehensive education?

12 'I would like to see the three members of the smokers' union whom I didn't have time to deal with yesterday. They can pay their dues in my room straight after assembly.' Devise two scenes that lead on from this request. One with a headteacher who looks back nostalgically on better days and another with a headteacher who takes a personal approach to the problem of young people smoking in school.

13 How does the school differ from the open space of fields in the play? What is Hines' intention in choosing the different locations in the play?

14 Anderson tells a very exciting story of an incident that happened to him and a friend. What is the difference between Anderson's and Casper's stories and how do you imagine the class react to each story?

15 In Billy's school, violence is normal. Some teachers appear to teach with violence – and it spreads to the boys who have bullying and fights.

If you were appointed the head of the school, how would you change it?

16 Is Billy capable of coping with life outside school? Has he failed or has his school failed?

17 Do other pupils get treated better than Billy? What about MacDowall and the young boy who brings the message to Mr Gryce's office?

18 Anderson tells a story about something he did as a young child. Write about an incident in your own childhood.

c) Animals

Billy's life is divided into home, school and experiencing nature with Kes. It is this part which is best teaching him something he enjoys and encouraging him to give something back.

19 What does Billy get from keeping Kes? Arrange a list and put them in an order with the most important first.

20 Do you think that Billy should have taken Kes from the nest and kept her captive?

21 Why do people keep pets? What different qualities do different animals have?

22 Try to find out about some of the more unusual pets people keep.

23 Would you draw any distinctions between animals which should be kept in captivity and those which shouldn't? Prepare to speak in a debate where the motion is:

'Keeping animals captive is cruel to them and in future all animals should be allowed to retain their independence.'

d) Right and wrong

24 Is Billy good or bad? He has been in trouble with the police. He steals from the library and his brother. Why does he do these things? Look at all the actions Billy does that might be considered wrong and discuss how Billy would defend them. Include:

Hitting Jud when he is drunk.
Taking a kestrel chick to rear and train.
Trespassing on the farmer's land.
Answering his mother back.
Taking Jud's betting money.
Stealing the library book.
Fighting MacDowall.

When you have considered Billy's reasons for these actions, decide whether he should have done them or not.

25 Find five positive or good actions that Billy does.

Billy is punished for coughing, daydreaming and not having a P.E. kit. Are these things that he should be punished for?

26 Has school been a good or bad influence on Billy?

27 Are Jud and Mum worse or better than the people at school? What are the good and bad things about Jud and Billy's mother?

28 When Jud kills Kes, Billy appeals to his mum to punish Jud, but she can't, simply because Jud is bigger than she is. If you could re-write the end of the play what do you think would be the fair thing to happen? Would Jud be punished, and if so how? Or would Billy get another hawk?

C In Performance

a) *Drama*

29 In Scene 2 we hear about The Firs, and the Estate (where Billy lives). In pairs, imagine you are people who live in either of these two districts and talk together about the people who live in the other district.

30 We don't always say what we are thinking. In groups of four read Scene 2 carefully. Then re-read the scene with one person playing Mr Porter and another Billy. The other pair speak the thoughts immediately after the line is heard. Then ask the questions again and open the discussion up to include the entire class.

31 In pairs take it in turns to tell a short story to the other. At first the person listening pays close attention, then half listens and finally stops listening altogether. Discuss how you both feel after this exercise. When does this happen to Billy in the play? What effect do you think it has on him?

32 Choose any moment from a scene in Billy's house that includes Billy, Jud and Mrs Casper. In groups of four, one person moulds the other three into a position that most effectively shows the attitude of each character and what is happening in the scene. Once everyone is frozen you can touch individuals on the shoulder and they must tell you how that character is feeling.

33 In fours, pretend to be the neighbours of the Casper household, who are gossiping about them. Select some overhead conversations about the family.

34 Read Scenes 15 and 17. Whilst two people read the text one sentence at a time, two others add the dialogue of Billy's conscience sitting on either shoulder and urging him to place the bet, or keep the money. Do you think it is a difficult decision for him?

35 In groups of four or more, improvise a scene where Mr Beal is talking to Mr Porter and other people, who live in the area, about the 'Casper family'. Make sure you are clear about how different characters feel about the family and the individuals within the family – Jud, Billy and Mrs Casper.

36 In pairs, take on the roles of Mr Sugden and Mr Farthing and show a spontaneous improvisation when they meet away from school in various locations, for example, a library, a pub, a betting shop, a football match, Billy's house and so on.

37 Working as a whole class, model one person into a statue of how Billy may be at the very end of the play. Make sure you are happy about how the person is positioned, hands, head, eyes. Each person in the class takes a role, either of a character in the play or someone like, for example, Billy's next door neighbour. Everyone approaches Billy one at a time and they say one sentence to Billy about how they feel about him and the dead kestrel. Build this exercise into a big tableau with all the characters of the play present, displaying the way they feel towards Billy.

b) Staging the play

Directing the action:

38 The stage direction at the beginning of Scene 19 says Jud
is 'very annoyed'. If this was not clear in the directions it
would not be obvious in the text. Think of other actions
and movements which could illustrate Jud's anger.

39 Read the section with Jud, Delamore and Gibbs in as many
ways as possible. Imagine the stage directions say 'very
happy', 'very suspicious', etc.

40 Dramatic irony is when the audience has information
which the actors on the stage do not share. Can you ident-
ify the dramatic irony in Act Two? What difference does it
make to the play? You may need to read from Scene 14
omitting Scenes 15 and 17 to really understand this.

41 In the final scene, the audience share with Jud and Billy
information not known to Mrs Casper. Would the scene
have been as successful if Mrs Casper had known about
the bet or the kestrel at the beginning of the scene?

42 How does the writer try to build a climax in the play
through Scene 19 to the end? Could the actors and director further develop this tension?

43 Scene 21 is the shortest in the play. What effect does having only a small amount of dialogue create? Think of this
scene as part of a film and try to write a camera script for
it. Imagine Billy in more than one location. Think about
long, medium and close-up shots. Are there times when
you would want to focus on parts of Billy's face, or hands?
Would you want to cut away to a scene somewhere else or
to other characters?

c) Designing the set and costumes

44 Make a list of all the images you think are important to the play – the school, the mine and so on.

45 Draw some simple sketches or take pictures from colour magazines to illustrate your images of the play and the set.

46 The play is set in a number of different scenes and it is not possible or desirable to provide a set for each location. List all the scenes, decide which you think may need more setting than others, try to keep the set to the minimum requirements for each scene.

47 Try to think of different ways of setting the play. Imagine different stages, arena (the audience all around), thrust (the audience on three sides) traverse (the audience on two sides). Discuss the advantages and disadvantages of these theatre spaces to the play.

48 When you have decided on one theatre space, design a set to work in that space. Keep it simple and concentrate on the images, atmospheres and feelings in the play.

49 Take two characters who interest you (not necessarily Billy, Jud or Mrs Casper). Using cut-outs from magazines invent costumes which best help the audience to understand their characters. If you choose Jud or Mrs Casper you may want to show the difference between the scenes at home and when they are going out.

OTHER TITLES IN THIS SERIES

Children's Ward   Age 12+

Paul Abbott, John Chambers and Kay Mellor
Granada TV

Six scripts from the popular Granada TV series Children's Ward. The plays trace the fortunes of patients admitted to the children's ward and the relationships between them.

Children's Ward also examines the way the programmes are made, and is an excellent medium for discussing the nature of television drama.

ISBN: 435 23285 1

Whose Life is it Anyway? Age 14+

Brian Clark

Whose Life is it Anyway? is both a powerful stage-play and major feature film about the struggle of the central character for the right to die.

Completely and permanently paralysed by an accident and dependent on a life-support machine, Ken Harrison challenges the traditional duty of the medical profession to keep him alive at all costs.

ISBN: 435 23287 8

Solomon's Cat

David Holman

A warm, lively play about a boy in Tanzania who joins up
with the local ranger to protect leopards from poachers. The
boy knows he is fighting to protect not only the leopards
but the future of wildlife in Tanzania so he takes incredible
risks. A topical and thought-provoking play from the author
of the best-selling **Whale**.

ISBN: 435 23297 5

The Wild Animal Song Contest and Mowgli's Jungle

Age 11+

Adrian Mitchell

Two lively plays which are ideal for classroom reading.

The Wild Animal Song Contest is a competion to see which animal from which country can produce the best song. Will it be Quilla the arrogant eagle from the US, or Raffa the timid giraffe from Africa? A funny and thought-provoking allegory of the world's nations. Adapted from Rudyard Kipling's The Jungle Book, **Mowgli's Jungle** centres on the boy's dilemma. Can Mowgli live as a man among people or should he return to the jungle as a wild boy?

ISBN: 435 23296 7

Two Men from Derby and Shooting Stars

Age 13+

Barry Hines

From the popular author of **Kes** come two plays on a
footballing theme which 13+ pupils will find enjoyable and
accessible.

For Freda, life as a miner's wife in the thirties is no joke.
When two men from Derby arrive hoping to sign her
husband up for Derby football team, she fantasises about
the chance to escape. But her husband doesn't come home
on time and as the men sit impatiently waiting, she sees her
dreams beginning to fade. In **Shooting Stars**, teenagers
from a poor neighbourhood kidnap their famous local
footballer and hold him to ransom. Calvin the footballer is
good-looking, rich and successful, but as Gary, Vic and
Sean sit guarding him, they discover that they all have
things in common.

ISBN: 435 23298 3

The Play of Cider with Rosie

Age 13+

Adapted by Nick Darke

This delightful dramatisation of Laurie Lee's boyhood memories is as fresh and youthful as the original. Loll's spirited escapades, the warmth and humour he finds in his family and the rich variety of characters in his Cotswold village are all brought vividly to life. This lively adaptation is an excellent play for classroom reading and performance.

ISBN: 435 23295 9

Joyriders
Age 14+
and Did You Hear the One About the Irishman?

Christina Reid

'Mighty Belfast' is the setting for these two plays by Belfast-born playwright, Christina Reid.

Joyriders is a hard-hitting play about four teenagers from the Divis flats in West Belfast. In **Did You Hear the One about the Irishman?** Alison and Brian's families are linked by marriage but deeply divided by religion. This edition has notes and assignments to help in meeting the requirements of Key Stage 4.

ISBN: 435 23292 4